IMAGES
*of America*

# TRINIDAD

This 1895 photograph shows a family in the open meadow of Ceremonial Rock, which stands in what is now Patrick's Point State Park. This ancient sea stack tells of a time before the land's rise above the waters that once covered it. From left to right are Mrs. Nevells, Mrs. Brooks, Mr. Brooks, Etta Brooks, an unidentified woman (standing), an unidentified man (seated), Tom Lee (16 years old), Gus Brooks, William Brooks, Lilly Brooks (with baby Charles), and Nan Brooks. (Courtesy HCHS.)

ON THE COVER: This undated photograph shows Dorothy and June Fountain looking out toward Trinidad Head. (Courtesy HSU.)

IMAGES
*of America*

# TRINIDAD

Dione F. Armand
with foreword by Ned Simmons

ARCADIA
PUBLISHING

Published by Arcadia Publishing
Charleston, South Carolina

Library of Congress Control Number: 2009930176

For all general information contact Arcadia Publishing at:
Telephone 843-853-2070
Fax 843-853-0044
E-mail sales@arcadiapublishing.com
For customer service and orders:
Toll-Free 1-888-313-2665

Visit us on the Internet at www.arcadiapublishing.com

*In memoriam, Bill Devall, who speaks for the trees—*

# CONTENTS

# FOREWORD

The redwood coast town of Trinidad is unique. The resulting photographic archives are a testament to this uniqueness, and when combined with historic documents, studies, and artistic interpretations, the distinctiveness of Trinidad is obvious.

I was asked to share some of my own rich personal history since my work and friendships go straight to the heart of the Trinidad region's history. This I can do in three words: "It was fated!"

From childhood, I wanted to work in the woods, and in 1960, I entered the forest management program at Humboldt State College. There I formed an early circle of friendships that cuts to the very core of this book with the Allen and Marian Horner family, Frances Purser, and Peter Palmquist. Allen's hobby was printing and he bought A. W. Ericson's equipment. While loading press type, Allen was asked to put boxes of photographic glass plates in the alley for the garbage man to pick up. Allen objected and instead the plates went to Frances, who received them for the college library. Peter Palmquist, the college photographer, was assigned to make prints from the plates. Many of the photographs in this book are from those saved glass-plate negatives.

Studying forestry during the 1960s at Humboldt State University was truly to be at the center of an epic battle. I was studying redwoods right after the 1950s logging binge and in the midst of the rising conflict between those who wished to continue to log at near-historic levels and those who wished to save the last of the ancient redwoods in the long-dreamed-of Redwood National Park. During that time, I attended meetings of the Society of American Foresters where I came to know many company foresters, including Al Merell, Herb Peterson, and Ed Mervich. During the same period, I attended Sierra Club potlucks where I developed friendships with Lucille Vinyard, Kay Chaffey, and Jean Hagood.

My first job post-degree was temporary, filling a beaches and parks position while their forester was on educational leave. A meaningful assignment was to go to Trinidad to meet with Joy Sundberg and Axel Lindgren Sr. to visit the Yurok village of Tsurai site. The parcel was subdivided and on the real estate market. My report was accepted and that was to be the end of my involvement with Tsurai.

Marian Horner introduced me to people interested in history and I was in another tight circle of friends that included Gwyneth Susan and Katie Boyle. We met in the home of Ruby McGregor and called our group Heritage Trinidad. Our project was to obtain landmark status for Tsurai. The Humboldt County Historical Society also supported the project, and Richard Harville, Andrew Genzoli, and Martha Roscoe also became my friends. In 1970, Tsurai became California Registered Historic Landmark No. 838.

I started teaching Trinidad History as an adult education class. Over 40 students enrolled and attendance was high. Attending class were Bruce Pettit, Ray Davis, Katie Boyle, and Charles Fleschner, who would later become charter board members of the Trinidad Museum Society. I like to think that I might have been a spark that lit a few torches.

By this time, I was employed by Western Timber Services as a timber cruiser measuring old growth timber in Redwood Creek during winter and mapping Sequoias in the Sierras during summer. I loved my work; my motto was "Every day a hike and every lunch a picnic." Between contracts I found part-time work such as land surveying or choker setting for a logger.

Next, I went to work on the maintenance crew of the new Redwood National Park. My skills were recognized and I assisted the Park Engineer in setting slope stakes for roads, parking lots, and the bridge at Lady Bird Johnson Grove, after which I was assigned to Stephen Veirs, the park biologist. At this time, I worked on forest fire history by dating fire scars and stumps and performing vegetation surveys. I also had an open-ended assignment to search for historical documents relating to the park and became proficient in Orick, Bald Hills, Klamath, and Crescent City history. While establishing an 800-foot buffer zone above the park boundary in Redwood Creek, I found the historic Trinidad Trail, which dates back to the gold rush. This spring, I was pleased to hear that the park archeologist followed my old flagging line marking the trail and filed a report.

In 1973, I finished my master's degree and obtained my professional forester license. I worked again for Western Timber Services as a consultant forester. I then became a forester for the Russ Ranch, 30,000 acres at the headwaters of Redwood Creek. The ranch contract logger was Harvey Paulsen. He was raised in the logging camps of Little River and we talked a lot about logging around Trinidad and how the stench of the whaling station accumulated in Crannell. Professionally, I was doing exactly what I wanted from childhood. It would be 16 years before I would have further direct involvement with Trinidad.

In Trinidad, a series of pivotal events were taking place. A meeting at town hall revealed that coastal land from Trinidad to Little River was to become a state park and that property condemnation orders were being issued. This was the first time most people had heard of the project and the community was galvanized against it. This led to the formation of three local nonprofit corporations: the Tsurai Ancestral Society, Humboldt North Coast Land Trust, and the Trinidad Museum Society.

In 1989, my world turned upside down. Divorced and diagnosed with a serious heart condition, the forest products market was depressed and I was broke. My response was to reinvent myself as an artist and poet. With money from my father, I bought a historic house in Trinidad and opened the front as a gallery: Trinidad Art. For 20 years now, I have been on the board of directors of both the Trinidad Museum Society (TMS) and the Humboldt North Coast Land Trust.

With Lindy Linberg and Carolyn Eisner, I helped Katie Boyle organize her large Trinidad photograph collection—a two-year project that became the basis of this book. In my research of Trinidad history, I was surprised to find my own family. The first schoolteacher in Trinidad was my great-grandmother's uncle, Charles King, who in 1870 became a wealthy man. He won the land lottery and cast his lot with the timber barons, including Joseph Russ. He was also part of the syndicate that purchased the timberlands of Redwood Creek, now part of Redwood National Park. Yes, my being in Trinidad was fated.

So too was finding the young historian Dione Armand, who was just returning from graduate study at Berkeley and writing her first book about a north coast redwood forest when she was introduced to me by my friend Joan Berman, librarian at Humboldt State University and fellow TMS board member. Dione's passion for the redwood region, beautiful writing style, and artistic sensibility combined with her knowledge of the region's history made her the perfect choice. She culled through hundreds of photographs to produce this volume and spent the past year working with the TMS and other local archives to offer this history of greater Trinidad.

Enjoy it and see you at Trinidad Art!

—Ned Simmons

# INTRODUCTION

Trinidad today is no less a magical place than it was in 1775 when the ships of Don Juan Francisco Bodega y Quadra and Don Bruno de Hezeta landed on her shores. Trinidad is, however, a place of changed magic. The Yurok village of Tsurai, whose community once greeted the Spaniards, is no longer there, nor is the ancient redwood forest. Instead the land shares its history in the timeless beauty of the landscape and in the continuing regeneration of families and forest alike. There are still to be found small remnants of historical events and structures of early Trinidad as well as the careful remembrances of families and the Trinidad Museum Society, which is dedicated to preserving Trinidad's history. When events, people, or historical landscapes or buildings are captured in an extant photograph, it is included in the present volume.

An unusually refracted view of the earliest inhabitants of Trinidad in the year 1775 is given to us by the unlikely voices of the Spanish explorers, in their royally-mandated journals. The expedition commander and captain of the *Santiago* (Hezeta), the captain of the *Sonora* (Bodega), the chaplain of the *Santiago* (Fray Miguel de la Campa), the vice commander of the *Santiago* (Pérez), and the second pilot of the *Sonora* (Mourelle) each give differing accounts of their 10-day visit. What the accounts have in common is their description of a verdant paradise overseen by native people who treat each other and the land with respect and restraint. They note the sturdy redwood plank homes, the animal skin and woven clothing, and the fine basketry of the inhabitants. They also note the giant trees, multiple clear springs, delicious fruits, berries, and mushrooms, and the recognizable landforms of Trinidad Head and of Little River, the latter of which they called *El Rio de las Tortolas* (River of Doves).

The meeting between the Spaniards and the Yurok started peaceably, but took a turn for the worse when two novice seamen defected from their party and the commander blamed the inhabitants of Tsurai. Hezeta's vicious attack on his hosts is described vividly in the Pérez account. It leaves no doubt that Tsurai's inhabitants would be left with an impression of white men as brutal and treacherous. Along with these tarnished memories, the Spanish also left a large wooden cross that they erected on Trinidad Head in the name of their king, Charles III. The fact that they held their ceremony on the Catholic feast day of the Holy Trinity led the Spanish to give Trinidad its present name. A replica of the cross, installed in 1913, can still be seen today.

Additional accounts come from explorer Captain Vancouver and his expedition's naturalist Archibald Menzies, and from explorer Don Francisco de Eliza in 1793. It was around this time that extant accounts turn to the fur trade, which was highly competitive around the turn of the century, and involved the activities of many recognized sovereign nations, most notably the Russians and the British. After the decimation of the sea otter population came the proverbial lull before the storm. Between 1817 and 1849, except for a couple of scattered reports, the Spaniard's cross at Trinidad Head stood unheralded and Tsurai and its inhabitants were able to live unimpeded, according to long-established traditions. However, in 1849, gold was discovered and at this point white incursion and settlement began in earnest.

In Carl Meyer's 1851 account of his time spent at Trinidad Bay, he writes, "It seemed as if a new harbor city had been called into being by the magic cry of gold." Indeed, after gold was discovered in 1849 near the Trinity River (so named because it was thought to lead to Trinidad Bay), a rush to find the old Spanish port led to an all-out search for the long-forgotten bay, which culminated in Trinidad's founding on April 8, 1850—making it the first established town in the Humboldt Bay region. Starting as a collection of tents, the new town of Trinidad was reported to have a population during the boom years of 1851–1852 of over 3,000 people, mostly miners, heading to or from the Trinity mines. This was not a stable population, especially as Arcata and Eureka became established ports. However, Trinidad for a time was the county seat of Klamath County and remained so until Klamath County became absorbed into Del Norte County to the north and Humboldt County to the south.

As Meyer had predicted in 1851, following gold mining, Trinidad quickly turned to mining the "red gold" of the redwoods and the timber trade became the predominant economic activity in the region. In the early days of logging, trees with the misfortune of growing near waterways were taken out first. Later, steam donkey yarding and railroads helped to speed the destruction of the forests well into the interior. Though this activity damaged entire watersheds and had a marked negative impact on salmon and other fish that depended on the clear cool waters of intact forests, the times were good for Trinidad. Logging provided steady work for hundreds of families. From 1851, when Baron Karl von Loeffelholz built a sawmill at Little River, to the heyday of modern industrial logging at Crannell, logging was the economic lifeblood of the town. Particularly prosperous were the families living in the Little River Redwood Company town of Crannell, just to the southeast of Trinidad. Many photographs of Trinidad logging and Crannell are included in this volume.

Since much of the timber coming out of the north woods was loaded onto ships at the port of Trinidad, it became critical that a lighthouse be built to increase the safety of maritime transportation. The Trinidad Head Lighthouse was erected in 1891 and is still active today. The fog bell house is the only remaining bell house in California.

Trinidad's importance as a maritime port also included a brief chapter in the history of commercial whaling. The time of the California Sea Products Company whaling station (1920–1927), places Trinidad in rare company as the home to one of the last whaling stations in the United States. The Blatt family's unusual and striking photographs of whaling aboard the SS *Hawk* whaling vessel provide a rich chronicle of that period in Trinidad's history.

In recent years, the city of Trinidad is experiencing a renaissance of sorts—a boom without a bust—since it is no longer based on the extraction of natural resources, but rather on the celebrated beauty and history of the town. Situated on a high bluff overlooking the Pacific Ocean, Trinidad today has become a popular tourist destination. It is home to the Humboldt State University Marine Laboratory as well as to a robust fishing industry. As a visitor today, you can see the replica of a traditional Yurok village at Sumêg in nearby Patrick's Point State Park. You can also visit the standing historic structures of the Holy Trinity Church and the Trinidad Museum, which are both examples of early Trinidad. In addition, as you walk around town, the street names evoke the gold rush ships and early settlers after which they are named. A short and pleasant walk up the trail onto Trinidad Head will bring you to the replica of the Spaniards' cross, placed there as a reminder of the history of Tsurai and Trinidad.

# ACKNOWLEDGMENTS

In this, my second book on Humboldt County history, I found great delight in the lively collaboration that brought it all together. For the countless discussions, reminiscences, shared fact-finding expeditions, and phone calls within our community, I say a heartfelt thank you to all. I would also like to express my deep gratitude to Joan Berman, special collections librarian at Humboldt State University and Trinidad Museum Society Board of Directors member, for her generous grant that made this book possible. Working with Ned Simmons has been an honor and a treat, both for his encyclopedic knowledge of greater Trinidad and for his charm. A thank you also goes to Patti Fleschner, president of the TMS Board, for her graciousness and for always knowing whom to call to keep lines of communication open. A heartfelt thank you to Allie Lindgren for her hospitality and for introducing me to the wonderful people of the Yurok Tribal Council. I am honored and humbled by the experience. In addition, Tom Sharp's warm assistance with Crannell's history and images was indispensable and a true delight. I would also like to thank all the local archives and their talented staffs that contributed their images and their considerable knowledge to this volume: the board of directors at the Trinidad Museum Society; Deborah Meador (research and collections manager), Linda DeLong (research center assistant), Durry Jones (executive director), and the board of directors at the Humboldt County Historical Society; Pam Service (curator) and Art Barab (registrar) at the Clarke Historical Museum; and Joan Berman (special collections librarian), Edie Butler (special collections assistant), and Rebekka Knierim (student intern) at Humboldt State University. Special thanks to my family and friends, who were endlessly patient with me while my thoughts were on Trinidad. In fact, since working on this volume, I find that Trinidad is like a second home to me—the light, the salt air and gentle earth, and most importantly, the people I have come to know and befriend. To Trinidad, such a lovely place, come one and all to visit and stay a while!

**Major Collection Names and Abbreviations**

Clarke Historical Museum (CL)
Humboldt County Historical Society (HCHS)
Humboldt County Historical Society, Lois Smith Collection (HCHS, LS)
Humboldt State University (HSU)
Humboldt State University, Roberts Collection (HSU, RC)
Humboldt State University, Schoenrock Collection (HSU, SC)
Trinidad Museum Society (TMS)
Trinidad Museum Society, Blatt Collection (TMS, BL)
Trinidad Museum Society, Katie Boyle Collection (HSU, KB)
Trinidad Museum Society, Tom Sharp Collection (TMS, TS)

# One

# EARLIEST INHABITANTS

Long before others arrived, the Yurok lived throughout the greater Trinidad region. Along the coast north and south of the Klamath River, and along the banks of the inland Klamath, Yurok people resided in permanent villages and made use of the abundant flora and fauna of the area. The southernmost coastal Yurok settlements were Sre-por on Little River and Tsurai (Chue-rey) on the shore of Trinidad Bay. By the time of the Spaniards' visit and misappropriation in 1775, the Yurok lived a lifestyle based on the abundance of the land around them. Ocean and river fishing served to sustain not only physical life, but spiritual and cultural life as well. To this day, relations between coastal Yurok (called Ner-'er-ner) and river Yurok both upriver and downriver are deep and abiding. Travel on established trails and by canoe on the Klamath River and the Pacific Ocean has always allowed for great mobility between neighboring communities, including the Tolowa to the north, the Wiyot to the south, and the Karuk to the east. Despite differences in language and geography, the people shared many cultural elements based on the centrality of the life-giving salmon. Tsurai village was abandoned in 1916, and Yurok lifeways were threatened by non-native settlement during the early years of the twentieth century. However, today Yurok life in Trinidad and the surrounding ancestral territory is vibrant and growing. The Yurok Tribe is currently the largest tribe in California, with more than 5,000 enrolled members.

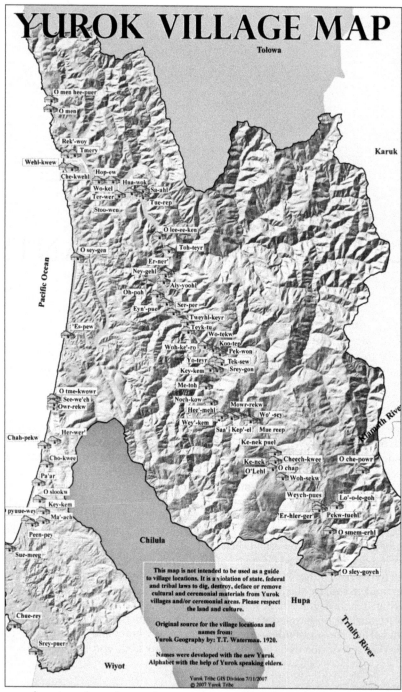

# YUROK VILLAGE MAP

Tolowa

Karuk

O men hee-puer
O men
Rek'-woy
Tmery
Wehl-kwew
Hop-ew
Che-kwehl
Haa-wok
Wo-kel
Sa-ahl
Ter-wer
Tue-rep
Stoo-wen

O lee-ee-ken
O sey-gen
Toh-teyr
Er-ner'
Ney-gehl
Aiy-yoohl
Oh-poh
Eyn'-pue
Ser-per
Tweyhl-keyr
'Es-pew
Teyk-tu
Wo-tekw
Koo-tep
Woh-ke'-ro
Pek-won
Yo-teyr
Tek-sew
Key-kem
Srey-gon
Me-toh
O tme-kwowr
Noch-kow
See-we'ch
Hee'-mehl
Mowr-rekw
Owr-rekw
Wo' -sey
Wey'-kem
San' Kep'-el Mue reep
Her-wer'
Chah-pekw
Ke-nek puel
Cho-kwee
Ke-nek Cheech-kwee O che-powr
Pa'ar
O'Lehl O chap
O slookw
Woh-sekw
Key-kem
Weych-pues
Lo'-o-le-goh
pyuue-wey
Ma'-ach
'Er-hler-ger' Pekw-tuehl'
Peen-pey
O smem-erhl
Chilula
Sue-meeg

This map is not intended to be used as a guide
to village locations. It is a violation of state, federal
and tribal laws to dig, destroy, deface or remove
cultural and ceremonial materials from Yurok
villages and/or ceremonial areas. Please respect
the land and culture.

O sley-goych

Hupa

Chue-rey

Original source for the village locations and
names from:
Yurok Geography by: T.T. Waterman. 1920.

Srey-puer

Names were developed with the new Yurok
Alphabet with the help of Yurok speaking elders.

Wiyot

Yurok Tribe GIS Division 7/11/2007
© 2007 Yurok Tribe

Pacific Ocean

Klamath River

Trinity River

Yurok ancestral territory hugs the northwestern coast of California both north and south of the Klamath River, and extends inland along the river banks toward its confluence with the Trinity River. The ancestral northern boundary is the Wilson Creek basin, south of Crescent City. The southern boundary is Little River, south of Trinidad. The landforms are diverse, with vast tracts of redwood and mixed coniferous forests, numerous waterways, prairies, and mountains. (Courtesy Yurok Tribe.)

This photograph of Tsurai village was taken by A. W. Ericson in 1906. It shows Tsurai in its final decade of Yurok habitation before the village was abandoned in 1916. At one time, it comprised a dozen redwood slab houses, a sweat house, water hole, brush-dance pit, graves, boat landing, and trails leading to and from the village. Shown are houses made of sawn lumber that replaced the original traditionally-built dwellings. The core of the village rested right above the beach, about 25 feet from the Pacific breaker line at the base of a coastal bluff half a mile east of Tsurewa (Trinidad Head). The hillside protected the people of Tsurai village from the wind, but there was no shelter to be found from the incursion of white settlers. (Courtesy HSU.)

This photograph from the early 1900s shows the traditional redwood plank dwellings of the Yurok village of Woh-sekw along the Klamath River. Using traditional tools such as wedges made of elk antler the Yurok would split the enormous trunks of wind-felled redwood trees into large straight-grained planks. Notice the vast redwood forest in the background. (Courtesy Yurok Tribe.)

This undated photograph shows the Tucker house, which, for many years, was the only house inhabited by a non-Yurok at the mouth of the Klamath. Tucker built the original house around 1876 when he arrived in Requa (Rek-woy). At left, the top of the tall rock known to the Yurok as Oregos can be seen. A Yurok story recounts that long ago the Klamath entered the ocean at Omen rather than at Requa and that no fish swam its waters. The Creator, seeing that the Yurok were hungry, moved the river's mouth to Requa and placed Oregos at the entrance as guardian. To this day, Oregos and Sister Rock across the channel guard the river and bring the fish in from the sea. (Courtesy HSU, RC.)

This is the house of Robert Spott of Requa, located on the south-facing hillside above the Klamath River. It is made of the traditional redwood planks and has one round entrance portal, just big enough for a person. Inside are places for sleeping, storage, and for a wood fire. (Courtesy TMS.)

This painting by Ned Simmons of Trinidad shows Robert Spott of Requa as a young man standing not far from his home near the mouth of the Klamath River with the crag Oregos in the background. Robert Spott's life (1888–1953) spanned a time when the pressures of white settlement, corporate logging, mining, and fishing were having a tremendously negative impact on the Yurok way of life. Spott, a young man from a high-ranking Yurok family, became a friend and informant to the UC Berkeley anthropologist A. L. Kroeber. (Courtesy Ned Simmons.)

This pre-1933 photograph of Requa shows the buildings owned by Robert Spott's adoptive father, Captain Spott. The hillside's lack of undergrowth and few trees date this photograph to during or slightly after the era when people used seasonal burning techniques to produce grass seed for food, as well as hazel twigs and grass for basket weaving. Seasonal burning helped to keep animal predators away from homes and livestock. By 1930, government entities such as the National Forest Service prohibited Yurok seasonal burning practices. (Courtesy of HSU, RC.)

This 1917 photograph shows Alice
Spott (Taylor), sister of Robert Spott,
with young Harry Roberts on the
bank of the Klamath River. The
Spott family had ancestral rights to
fish nearby. (Courtesy HSU, RC.)

This c. 1926 photograph shows, from
left to right, Adeline, Evelina, and
Edith McCovey. (Courtesy HSU, RC.)

This photograph by J. A. Meiser shows Captain Spott, the adoptive father of Robert Spott. Captain Spott's father was born at Omen Hipur and his mother was a doctor from Requa. At a young age he started a freight service, hauling goods and people between Requa and Crescent City by canoe. (Courtesy HSU, SC.)

This undated photograph shows Tsurai Oscar with his parents, Old Tsurai and Mrs. Old Tsurai (full name unknown), who lived in Tsurai near Old Mau, the venerated elder who was the village's final leader before it was abandoned in 1916. (Courtesy TMS, KB.)

This undated postcard photograph shows a house built into the hollowed out base of a giant redwood tree at Prairie Creek, which is now part of Redwood National and State Parks. Redwoods can be hollow at the base from repeated fires and still continue to thrive. Locally, these trees are referred to as goosepens. (Courtesy TMS.)

This photograph shows the upper lattice of a dance pit (back right) and a sweat house in Sumêg at Patrick's Point State Park, just north of Trinidad. The sweat house structure consists of a room underground, which has two doors—one for entering and the other for exiting. The redwood slab roof allows for venting the wood fire smoke. The sweat house is used by men and boys for sleeping, bathing, and ritual purification, and occasionally by medicine women. (Courtesy Dione F. Armand.)

This photograph is of Captain Jack of Requa in 1926. He is shown here singing and playing the square double-headed frame drum, also known as a gambling drum. During a Yurok gambling game, the singer's team is said to gain a psychological advantage due to the singing accompanying the game. (Courtesy of HSU, RC.)

Fanny Flounder of Espeu (Es-pew), born in 1870, was a famous Yurok doctor. From the deck of her redwood house, which was built high up on a sea-facing bluff, Fanny looked down almost vertically to the mouth of the Klamath River. One day, as she watched, the ocean broke through the bar that the river had built up. Fanny shook her head and said, "You see what happens. The earth tips so far that the ocean spills into the river. Whales will come up the river! And all this is because there are no longer enough Yurok people left. When there were many of my people they danced and sang stamping their feet hard on the earth. This kept the earth from tipping and the ocean from flowing into the river." (Courtesy of HSU, RC.)

In order to gather mussels and hunt sea lions, as well as to travel on river and ocean waters, the Yurok build large dugout canoes from the wood of a single redwood tree. Learning to recognize a good "canoe tree" takes training and experience. It also does not kill the tree. Trees are revered as sacred and most traditional uses of redwood are carefully performed with the least impact on forest lands. (Courtesy TMS.)

This *c.* 1920s photograph by Ruth K. Roberts shows a Yurok grandmother and grandson on the Klamath River in a traditional hand-hewn double-header canoe made entirely of redwood. (Courtesy HSU, RC.)

Axel Lindgren Jr. and a helper are shown in 1970 fashioning a canoe from a single redwood tree. Yurok canoes are not deep, but are wide and long. Fashioning with hand tools is an arduous and lengthy process. The basic shape of the canoe is formed by chiseling, burning, and scraping the tree after it has been split, and then turned flat-side down so that the strong heartwood forms the bottom of the canoe. As it reaches its final shape, the canoe becomes light enough to travel on water. (Courtesy TMS.)

An all-Yurok crew constructed a replica of the original village of Sumêg at Patrick's Point State Park in 1990. This photograph shows the plank structure of a traditional redwood house lashed together using hazel saplings that have been made into fibers by heating, soaking, and twisting into strong rope. Notice the edges of the planks, which bear the marks of hand tools. (Courtesy Dione F. Armand.)

This photograph shows the dance pit at Sumêg at Patrick's Point State Park. Traditionally, if a family has a sick child, they take apart their plank home to create a pit for a brush dance. The brush dance is a healing spiritual ceremony and social event that takes place over several days. (Courtesy Dione F. Armand.)

Surf fishing is an important activity for coast Yurok fishermen. Surf fish school in shallow waters near the shore. They feed on plankton and in turn become food for seabirds, marine mammals, and a variety of fishes, including salmon. (Courtesy TMS, TS.)

This undated photograph shows a baby cradled in a traditional Yurok carrying basket on the beach near Tsurai with children and a dog. (Courtesy HCHS, LS.)

This photograph of Bob Peters fishing near Trinidad was taken by Edward Curtis in 1923. (Courtesy Library of Congress.)

This early 1900s photograph by Edward Curtis shows a Yurok man fishing in the river with a dip net. Notice that he holds the cord of the net in his right hand. Once the fish enter the net, he pulls the cord to entrap the fish before pulling the full net out of the water. The relationship between Yurok and fish, particularly salmon, encompasses much more than the Western view of wildlife as a food resource. The Yurok maintain a sacred and deliberate relationship with fish and forest, which are recognized as sacred beings. Traditionally salmon are allowed to pass upriver for a half moon before any are caught. This leaves the strongest to spawn and allows for the continued vibrancy of river life. The balance and restraint fostered by Yurok tradition is at odds with continuing pressure from logging impacts and upriver farming. This struggle to keep river water for the salmon continues today. (Courtesy of Library of Congress.)

This 1915 photograph shows Annie Kirby, half-sister of Eliza Lindgren, next to Luffenholtz Creek with surf fish. Axel Lindgren tells of when, in 1903, Annie and her husband George were evicted from their southern Tsurai village home by a sheriff and two Little River Redwood Company men and told never to return. Those Tsurai homes that were within the city limits of Trinidad fared a bit better, but by 1907, only 12 families remained in Tsurai, and by 1916, the village was abandoned. (Courtesy HCHS, LS.)

This 1951 photograph shows Aileen Figueroa, daughter of Maggie Pilgrim and singer and master teacher of Yurok language, turning surf fish at Luffenholtz Beach to aid in the drying process. The dried grasses laid beneath the fish also aid in the drying. (Courtesy TMS, KB.)

This 1951 photograph shows Kathleen Figueroa and a friend washing surf fish in a handmade Yurok basket at Luffenholtz Beach. The open work basket allows fish to spawn. The fact that the net is turned away from the water indicates that she is finished. (Courtesy of TMS, KB.)

This c. 1910s photograph shows a Yurok woman laying out surf fish to dry at the base of the bluffs at Luffenholtz Beach. (Courtesy of the HCHS, LS.)

26

Maggie Pilgrim is shown here in 1964 weaving traditional Yurok baskets. The "111" tattoo on her chin indicates her high-ranking family status. (Courtesy TMS, KB.)

This 1905 photograph shows Skarap weaving a storage basket. As was customary at the time, she is also referred to by her second husband's name as Mrs. Humpback Jim. Skarap was born at Herwer, a village at Stone Lagoon. Humpback Jim was from Weitchpec (Weych-pues) and came to Tsurai to marry Skarap. Their home was near the sacred pepperwood tree. (Courtesy TMS, KB.)

This photograph shows Trinidad Pete and his wife, Emma, two of the last inhabitants of Tsurai before the village was abandoned in 1916. (Courtesy TMS, KB.)

This *c.* 1910s photograph shows Trinidad Pete standing while Dora James works with the surf fish drying in the sun. Men caught the fish and the women had the important responsibility of processing the fish once caught. (Courtesy HCHS, LS.)

This photograph shows Trinidad Pete on Luffenholtz Beach mending a dip net. The dip nets in use by coastal Yurok along the surf line are constructed with a long triangular wooden frame that is held at the narrow end so that the wide end can be placed in the surf. The net is strung around this frame, and because it is long at the upper end, fish can be caught and then shifted, allowing multiple dips of the net in successive waves. (Courtesy TMS, KB.)

This photograph shows a traditional Yurok salmon roast in contemporary Trinidad. A pit about 15 feet long and a yard wide is banked with logs and ringed by dozens of slender stakes around the fire's perimeter. The stakes are stuck into the sandy ground and slabs of salmon are spitted onto them. Yurok men handle every aspect of the barbecue: wood gathering, fishing for and filleting the fish, making the barbecue stakes, and roasting the salmon. The man shown is unidentified. (Courtesy TMS, KB.)

This early-1900s photograph shows Charlie Beach on Luffenholtz Beach with his surf-fishing net laying on the ground behind him. His uncle, Axel Lindgren Sr., was an expert in net making, using nylon netting and tanoak dye. Traditional nets are made of two-ply cordage of hand-rolled fibers from the *Iris macrosiphon* leaf. Women gather the plant materials and roll the fibers into string, and men knot the nets. The mesh spacer and shuttle is made of elk antler and net weights are made with grooved, pierced, or naturally perforated stone. This type of net is still in use today. (Courtesy TMS, KB.)

This 1920s photograph shows medicine woman Eliza Warren (Lindgren) of Tsurai (at right) and Kittie Jack. Because of her powers, Lindgren was often called upon for assistance. If fishing or hunting was poor, she gathered Douglas fir branches, herbs, and roots to make medicine from them, and then used the medicine during prayer over the hunter's gun or the fisherman's tackle. Good hunting or fishing was sure to resume. (Courtesy TMS, KB.)

This 1919 photograph taken by Axel Lindgren Sr. shows the Lindgren family together at Old Home beach in 1919. From left: Frances, William (holding Axel Jr.), their mother Georgia, and Louisa. (Courtesy Lindgren Family.)

Axel Lindgren Sr. built a home for his family on the Lindgren property on a bluff overlooking the Pacific Ocean. This 1938 photograph shows the house under construction in the background while family and friends pose for a quick snapshot. From left to right are the following: (front row) Dally Lindgren, Allie Lindgren, Lena Mae Taylor, Joann Dobrec, and Maureen Cull; (back row) Bobby Cull, Tiny Lindgren, and Wilda Lindgren Gallacci. (Courtesy Lindgren Family.)

This *c.* 1915 photograph shows Fannie Gaston (Riecke), second wife of August "Gus" Riecke (1870–1930), one of the four sons and seven daughters of Trinidad pioneers August and Marie Helene Riecke, who in 1870 came to Trinidad via San Francisco from Germany. Fannie was born in the Yurok village of Kawtep (Koo-tep) in 1888. She married August after his first wife, Elizabeth Billy "Blind Lizzie" of Tsurai, passed away. Fannie and August were married in 1915 in Requa, and they had three children (Gertrude "Gertie" Riecke, Leslie Riecke, and August "Gussie" Riecke) before her untimely passing in 1920. (Courtesy Riecke Family.)

This *c.* 1911 photograph shows Alexander "Sandy" Childs of Trinidad, son of Willie Childs of Tsurai and William Childs, a major landholder in early Trinidad. Childs also operated a store and served as postmaster. (Courtesy TMS, KB.)

Axel Lindgren Sr. taught himself the fine art of whittling intricate fans out of cedar wood. Each fan piece is whittled individually and is then tied together. He is shown here in 1970 with one of his creations. (Courtesy Lindgren Family.)

This c. 1908–1914 photograph shows Minnie Wendler (Floyd) at right with first husband, Charles "Happy" Floyd, and her friend Maude Stewart at Big Lagoon. Minnie and her second husband, Leonard T. Natwick, operated the Korbel Hotel until 1949. (Courtesy Riecke Family.)

This 1952 photograph shows Georgia Lindgren, wife of Axel Sr., holding her grandson, Joe Lindgren, in her arms. Georgia was born in Weitchpec in 1894 and moved to Trinidad when she was 16 years old. (Courtesy Lindgren Family.)

Axel Lindgren Sr. is shown here at the Lindgren family property in 1970 playing the violin that once belonged to his father, Capt. Charles Lindgren, a Swedish sea captain. Not shown is the redwood tree on the Lindgren property from which Axel made a 16-foot dugout canoe. Around 1907, Axel fished commercially with longtime friend, Gus Riecke. (Courtesy Lindgren Family.)

# Two

# OLD TOWN TRINIDAD

Old town Trinidad, covering the period of initial non-native settlement in 1850 and extending nearly a century until just after World War II, was in many ways typical of other towns in the new state of California. First the gold rush and then the Homestead Act fueled white settlement in the greater Trinidad region. The federal government was expanding its boundaries "from sea to shining sea" by providing land incentives to white settlers and resource-hungry capitalists. Men came from far and wide to make a living from the vast near-wilderness frontier. In the far reaches of northern California, Trinidad became the first non-native settlement to be founded in the Humboldt Bay region. The town was founded on April 8, 1850, and held its first election on April 13. By June of that year, Trinidad had attracted a non-native population of 300 and, due to its importance as a base for miners heading to and from the Trinity mines, the population quickly climbed to over 3,000. Trinidad's location made it an important regional hub for mining, logging, whaling, salmon fishing, and maritime transportation of people and goods. The old town center was first located down near Trinidad Bay and later moved up to the bluffs above the bay. With the construction of the Redwood Highway, the town center moved again to maximize its proximity to motorists. Fire was a regular visitor to Trinidad; major fires in 1871, 1926, 1928, and 1945 caused older structures to be replaced with new ones by the town's resilient citizens. Today the names of early pioneer families and gold rush-era ships can be seen in the names of the streets. Trinidad history has been carefully recorded and preserved by the Trinidad Museum Society.

This 1909 engraving by S. Hollyer depicts the popular view of a Spanish galleon arriving in what was to them a new world. Spanish ships entered the bay that they later named Trinidad on June 9, 1775, and remained for 10 days. Capt. George Vancouver of Great Britain arrived on May 2, 1793, for a three-day visit. One additional Spanish ship made a brief visit in August 1793. (Courtesy Library of Congress.)

This c. 1890–1910 photomechanical print by W. H. Lippincott depicts the popular view of Spaniards arriving on the shores of North America to claim land for the Spanish crown. The Christian cross shown is typical of European expansionist practice. The cross, with its implication of divine providence, brought with it claims of Christian dominion. The fact that native people already inhabited the land was not respected. (Courtesy Library of Congress.)

During their 10-day visit to Yurok territory in June 1775, personnel on the Hezeta expedition's three ships wrote accounts of their experiences. One account states that two days after their arrival, "the commandant took possession of those lands with all the dignity and solemnity that the accommodations of the port afforded, mass was celebrated, a sermon was preached, and many volleys of cannon and guns were fired as an act of thanks to the Creator." The chaplain describes that together the men sang "*Te Deum Laudamus*," and then ascended the steep path to place a cross on Trinidad Head. Because the date was the first day of the Catholic Feast of the Holy Trinity, the Spaniards christened the port Trinidad. Shown is the 1913 granite monument of the Spaniards' cross. (Courtesy HSU.)

THE WAY THEY GO TO CALIFORNIA.

This lithograph from 1849 makes fun of the hysteria that ensued in California after the discovery of gold was announced. In 1845, Major Reading arrived at a river previously unknown to explorers that he named the Trinity because he mistakenly thought that it emptied into Trinidad Bay. In 1848, he returned to the Trinity and found gold, a discovery that led to the California gold rush. Even though the bay was prominently marked on Spanish maps, it had not been located in many years by land or sea. In 1849, two parties left the Trinity mines to find Trinidad Bay. One traveled south to San Francisco to prepare to search for Trinidad by ship. The other, the Josiah Gregg expedition, attempted to find an overland route. By land and sea, the Trinidad harbor proved difficult to find. The furor over finding the elusive harbor was such that in the month of March 1850 there were no less than 11 vessels leaving from San Francisco to find it. Two of those ships, the *California* and the *Laura Virginia*, were successful in finding Trinidad Bay. (Courtesy Library of Congress.)

This view shows Trinidad on the bluff above Trinidad Bay and the cows crossing the pasture at the base of Trinidad Head as they did every evening. Notice the stacks of lumber in the foreground. The first sawmill within the greater Trinidad region was operated south of Trinidad at Luffenholtz Creek by Baron Karl von Loeffelholz from 1851 to 1854. (Courtesy HCHS.)

This A. W. Ericson photograph was taken in the 1890s and shows the McConnaha Shingle Mill to the left and the two spurs of the Ryder Wharf railway. One forks toward the original Old Town Trinidad, and the other to the Hooper Brothers mill at Mill Creek (established in 1853 by Deming and March) located on the bluff over what is now Trinidad State Beach. In 1883, the Hooper Brothers sold the mill at Mill Creek and their other mill south of town to the California Redwood Company syndicate. (Courtesy HSU.)

This photograph by A. W. Ericson shows Trinidad as it appeared in 1893 from the headland. In the center is the white Occidental Hotel with the Brick Store behind it. The only building shown that exists today is the Catholic church in the upper right. (Courtesy HCHS.)

This photograph shows Trinidad's second commercial center, located along the old stagecoach road (today East Edwards Street). Pink's Saloon on the corner of Mallory (now Trinity) and Edwards Streets is visible. Also pictured are the Billy Beach Barber Shop, Pinkham's Hotel, McConnaha's General Merchandise, and the Chaffey house. The Trinidad Hotel stands at the far right. The unpainted building at center is Sangster's Store. (Courtesy TMS, KB.)

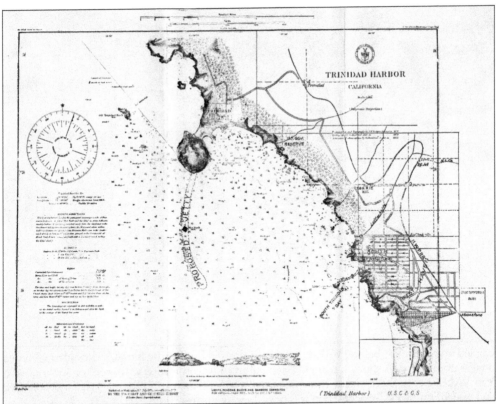

In 1879, Charles G. Yale declared in a pamphlet that since there had been 427 shipping disasters on the northern coast, there should be a harbor of refuge built between San Francisco and the Columbia River. Yale campaigned for Trinidad Bay, which was already protected on one side by the 375-foot high Trinidad Head. His unsuccessful proposal was to build a breakwater to enclose one square mile of anchorage. Harbor improvements to the south at Humboldt Bay began in 1889. (Courtesy HCHS, LS.)

This photograph shows the steamer *Saint Paul* in 1895. The passenger-freight vessel's route was San Francisco to Astoria, with Trinidad as a port of call. On the fogged-in night of October 5, 1905, the *Saint Paul* was headed north off the coast of Punta Gorda when it struck some rocks. All 93 passengers and 60 officers and crew members were rescued, but the ship sank irretrievably in the waters of the Pacific. (Courtesy CL.)

Copied from a tintype before 1870, this image of the Old Brick Store is one of the oldest recorded images of Trinidad. It shows a team of oxen pulling a wagon loaded with wool on Golindo and Van Wyke Streets. Stores at the time were usually general merchandise stores that also sold feed and grain. Sangster's Tobacco Shop was next door. (Courtesy TMS, KB.)

This 1907 photograph shows the Trinidad Post Office when it was in the Underwood Store at the corner of Edwards and Trinity Streets. There were no post offices in the Trinidad area until 1853. Instead, mail was carried by private express companies that charged high rates. The first express was started by A. E. Ragnes in the spring of 1851 and ran between Trinidad and the mines near Bestville, a distance of over 100 miles. (Courtesy TMS, KB.)

In 1904, Clarence John McConnaha took over a general merchandise store in Trinidad that had been previously owned and operated in the brick building by Philetus Bell, brother of Josiah Bell. The store was sold to Webster and Chaffey in 1914. Note the two gas lamps on the street. (Courtesy HSU.)

This early-1900s photograph shows the C. J. McConnaha General Merchandise Store at the corner of Edwards and Trinity Streets in Trinidad. Glenn Chaffey is shown on far left. He was later killed in World War I. The house shown to the right was later occupied by the Saunders family. Two doors down and across the street stood the Underwood Store, and Pinkham's Saloon was on the corner. (Courtesy TMS, KB.)

This photograph shows the Webster and Chaffey Store, which was purchased from C. J. McConnaha in 1914. Just after World War I, Mose Saunders came to Trinidad to pay tribute to his fallen Army friend, Glenn Chaffey, and immediately fell in love with Glenn's sister Mae. The two were married in 1923; in 1924, their son Glenn was born. (Courtesy TMS, KB.)

This undated photograph shows George Pinkham (left) and Warren Watkins with their catch. George Pinkham was married to Charlotte "Lotte" Riecke and owned the Pinkham Saloon. Pinkham and the Riecke family were also good friends with A. W. Ericson. Watkins and his wife Rose Sangster (Watkins) operated the Occidental Hotel. (Courtesy Riecke Family.)

This September 1912 photograph shows the interior of the Underwood Store at Edwards and Trinity Streets. Pictured from left to right are Martha Underwood, Maude Harrington (Hunter), and Jane Childs. Notice the display of Yurok baskets on the center table. (Courtesy TMS, KB.)

This pre-1900 photograph by G. W. Miller shows the interior of Alexander "Sandy" Sangster's tobacco shop. The shop was located near the Old Brick Store and the Occidental Hotel on Golindo and Van Wycke Streets. (Courtesy TMS, KB.)

This photograph shows Trinidad along the Old Redwood Highway in 1928. At left is the Trinidad Garage and next to it the Saunders Store. On the right (not shown), is the Big Four Inn. (Courtesy TMS, KB.)

This 1893 photograph by A. W. Ericson shows the steamer *Emily* loading at Trinidad Wharf. Trinidad was an important port of call for a steamship line between San Francisco and Oregon. Notice the huge boom for hoisting cargo at the far end of the wharf. This photograph was taken not long before the wharf was abandoned. (Courtesy HSU.)

This postcard from the first decade of the 20th century by A. W. Ericson shows the Trinidad Hotel at the east end of Edwards Street. A. W. Ericson is shown standing in front of the hotel. (Courtesy TMS, KB.)

This photograph shows the Hooper Brothers Store in Trinidad where A. W. Ericson worked as a clerk (1874–1876) before he became a photographer. His diary records that in September 1871, he took the Hooper Brothers' schooner *Lola* from San Francisco to Trinidad, a journey of three days under favorable conditions. The *Lola* carried lumber and shingles as well as passengers. It was wrecked in January 1878. (Courtesy TMS, KB.)

This undated photograph looks northward on Trinity Street at the many automobiles parked near the Ocean View Hotel. (Courtesy TMS, KB.)

This undated photograph by G. H. Par shows workers inside the McConnaha Garage on Main Street in Trinidad. Greta Taynton (McConnaha) reported that, "At one time, practically everybody in Trinidad was employed by the McConnaha Brothers Company." (Courtesy TMS, KB.)

This photograph shows Axel Lindgren Sr. working at McConnaha's Shingle Mill in Trinidad. He called this work "tripping bolts." In 1910, C. J. McConnaha bought a 314-acre ranch at Martin's Ferry. He built a sawmill there and began to cut and mill the timber. The lumber his mill produced was used to construct the bridges at Martin's Ferry, Orleans, and Weitchpec. That same year, C. J. and his brother Burr also opened a shingle mill in Trinidad. (Courtesy TMS, KB.)

This 1910 photograph shows boys playing ball at the first Trinidad School, which was located by the Trinidad Cemetery. In 1914, the old school was abandoned and a new school was built on a new four-acre site. This second school served the community well until it burned down in 1949. (Courtesy TMS, KB.)

Charles B. Ryder's wharf on Trinidad Head was completed in August 1859, at a cost of $8,000. Along its length ran a railway with cars drawn by mules or oxen. Rusted rails can still be seen today hanging down from the cut in the rocks made for the wharf's construction. (Courtesy TMS.)

This early-1900s photograph is from the same vantage point as an 1894 image taken by A. W. Ericson from a window in the Occidental Hotel at the foot of Golindo Street. Notice the sandy area in front of Little Head. The sand was removed in the 1940s. The wharf along Trinidad Head appears in a state of disrepair. (Courtesy TMS.)

This photograph shows A. W. Ericson around 1925 in the redwoods. Ericson was the most prominent photographer in Humboldt County from about 1885 until his death in 1927. He came to Trinidad in 1869, and long before he started photographing woodsmen, he worked among them as an edger at the Hooper Brothers Mill in Trinidad. Later he worked as a clerk at the Hooper Brothers Store. It is likely that his interest in photography started when he served as a guide to photographers N. B. Strong and Edgar Cherry during their tour through timberlands in the area from Trinidad to Hoopa in 1881–1882. Although he lived in Trinidad from 1869 until his move to Arcata in 1877, Ericson was not creating photographs at that time. As Peter Palmquist said, "Given my druthers, I would wish that Ericson started photography at a far earlier time. How fine it would be if he had made a series of photographs showing every aspect of life in Trinidad since his arrival." (Courtesy HSU.)

This photograph shows a Trinidad home on Main Street built in 1870 that is reputed to be the home of "Cockeyed" Florence, a notorious woman of ill repute. Every year, Trinidad hosts a parade to the Trinidad Cemetery in her honor. Across the street stood a livery stable and a stagecoach stop. (Courtesy TMS, KB.)

This undated photograph shows a group of motorists in Trinidad posing with their automobiles. Notice the dress hanging over the rightmost car's grill. (Courtesy TMS, KB.)

This 1891 photograph shows a picnic taking place in Trinidad with Trinidad Head and Trinidad Bay in the background. (Courtesy TMS.)

This undated photograph shows the house of the Riecke family on Trinity Street (now Trinidad Art), which was built by Warren Watkins Jr., who also built the Sangster-Underwood house (now the Trinidad Museum). Julia Gertrude "Gertie" Riecke is shown standing in the side yard. (Courtesy Riecke Family.)

This early-1900s photograph shows the interior of the Good Templar Hall on Hector Street near Edwards. It was later moved to the corner of Main Street and Scenic Drive and became a café and bar called "The Big Four." In 1881, the Good Templar Lodge was described as owning its own hall and the adjacent lots and as doing "much noble work in the community." (Courtesy TMS, KB.)

On September 6, 1913, the Federated Women's Clubs of Humboldt County pulled aside a Stars and Stripes veil to reveal a new monument made by L. M. Klepper out of a single block of Rocklin white granite. This still-standing monument reaches 12 feet from base to tip and is a replica of the cross that the Hezeta expedition placed on Trinidad Head in 1775. The south-facing inscription reads: "*Carolus III Dei G Hyspaniarum Rex* / Charles III, by the Grace of God, King of Spain." (Courtesy HSU.)

Rose Sangster came to Trinidad in 1863 with her husband, Jabez, and sons James and Sandy. Her voyage from San Francisco took 29 days in rough seas. In 1865 her husband died, leaving her with two sons plus a daughter, Kristina. She soon started her own hotel, known as the Occidental Hotel. She married Warren Watkins and they had two children. In 1871, her first hotel burned down and she built another in its place. (Courtesy HSU.)

This undated photograph was found in the Susie Baker Fountain Papers. The building at center is Pinkham's Saloon. Susie Baker Fountain, Humboldt State University's first graduate in 1915, was a local historian and professional columnist for the *Blue Lake Advocate*. She developed an extraordinary clipping file and collection of materials on Humboldt County and Del Norte County people, activities, and history from 1850 to 1966. (Courtesy HSU.)

In 1945, the Hallmark Fisheries Company built a 575-foot pier at Trinidad Harbor. Little Head sits to the left of the pier. Spanish Rock and Prisoner Rock are visible offshore. (Courtesy TMS, KB.)

This 1872 photograph of Houda's Landing shows the edge of the high-line crane that lowered pallets of redwood shingles to waiting steamships below. Offshore at nearby Honda Cove, ships could drop anchor to receive their payload. Camel Rock (also known as Little River Rock) sits 100 yards offshore. Today, Camel Rock supports large breeding colonies of sea birds. (Courtesy HCHS, LS.)

This unusual early-1900s photograph shows a man fixing his fishing net at the base of the bluff not far from Little Head in Trinidad. (Courtesy CL.)

This photograph shows the stage coach and four-horse team of the McConnaha Brothers Stage. Burr McConnaha ran the stage line from Trinidad to Requa. Among those who drove for the McConnaha Brothers were Everett Griffin, Emery Thompson, Johnny More, Holger Kring, Ray Graham, Frank Epps, Ed Nellist, and Charles Delamore. (Courtesy TMS, KB.)

This photograph shows the corner of Edwards and Trinity Streets before the fire of 1928. A cow barn, Pink's Saloon, Billy Beach Barber Shop, and C. J. McConnaha's General Merchandise are shown. Jim Blue is shown standing next to the gas light with "Fisherman Dave" Nesbith (left) and Billy Beach (right). Others are unidentified. (Courtesy TMS, KB.)

This photograph shows the Trinidad Quarry near the Trinidad Rail Depot. During the construction of the North Jetty across the bay from Eureka, much of the required rock was hauled from the Trinidad Quarry by rail to the construction site at the far end of Samoa. (Courtesy HSU.)

58

The Hammond Lumber Company built a railroad from Samoa on the Humboldt Bay inland to Fieldbrook and this line was gradually extended to Trinidad between 1902 and 1906. The Hammond Lumber Company sold the railroad to the Southern Pacific Railroad Company on July 1, 1911. The Trinidad to Eureka portion of the tracks became a part of the Northwestern Pacific Railroad. The line transported mostly forest products such as logs, shingles, and milled lumber. (Courtesy HCHS.)

Passenger train service to and from Trinidad was announced to an excited public in 1907. The line that became known as the Northwestern Pacific Railroad took over passenger service in 1911. The company stopped running passenger trains to and from Trinidad by 1930. However, the Redwood Empire Route would continue to run from Eureka to points south for many years. (Courtesy HCHS.)

This early-1900s photograph shows the Trinidad Rail Depot in its heyday. During this period, it was possible to buy a ticket from Eureka to Trinidad. The passenger left Eureka on the steamer *Antelope*, caught the Northwest Pacific train at Samoa, and finally arrived at the Trinidad Rail Depot. (Courtesy HCHS.)

In 1880, the Trinidad Mill Company purchased a Baldwin locomotive to transport timber from their 10,000 acres of virgin redwood timberlands. The locomotive's original name *Sequoia* was changed to *Trinidad* when it was sold in 1887 to the Elk River Railroad Company. It was hauled out of Trinidad by wagon, only to become stuck in the sands of Clam Beach. Eventually serving on the South Jetty and in Elk River, the engine was retired in 1934. (Courtesy TMS, KB.)

This photograph shows the Holy Trinity Catholic Church at Parker and Hector Streets in a state of disrepair. The church was built in 1873, eventually fell into disuse, and was later restored. (Courtesy TMS, KB.)

This *c.* 1896 photograph shows the Riecke family at the beach in Trinidad. Charlotte Riecke is shown at center with her sister, Gertrude, seated in front of her. Both are wearing bangs. Marie Helene Riecke is shown wearing a hat and wrapped with a blanket. (Courtesy Riecke Family.)

This c. 1905 photograph shows a group assembled in Trinidad for a turkey shoot. George William Pinkham is pictured at center right holding his rifle with the barrel up. His wife, Charlotte Riecke Pinkham, sits next to him. (Courtesy Riecke Family.)

This undated photograph of children on driftwood in Trinidad is from the Gwyneth Susan collection. Susan is the great-granddaughter of Rose Sangster, who came to Trinidad in 1863 from Wisconsin by way of San Francisco. (Courtesy HSU.)

# *Three*

# Trinidad Head Lighthouse

As the gold rush slowed and the milling of the "red gold" of north coast redwoods accelerated, Trinidad became an important mill town with many ships using the fog-enshrouded bay. In 1854, a lighthouse was proposed, and 42 acres were purchased for that purpose in 1866. On February 15, 1871, it was announced that the Light House Board had decided to move forward on a project to erect a fourth-class light on Trinidad Head. Col. R. S. Williamson chartered the steamtug *H. H. Buhne* to convey him from Eureka to Trinidad. After rejecting Pilot Rock as a suitable location, he chose a site on the headland above the town of Trinidad. The light was to be placed at a height of 250 feet above the level of the ocean. Material and machinery for the new light would be transported by the McConnaha's schooner *Lola* and Jeremiah Kiler was appointed Head Keeper. The Trinidad Head Lighthouse was officially put into service on December 1, 1871, when Kiler activated the revolving fourth-order Fresnel lens for the first time. The lighthouse's coal-oil lantern required constant tending to keep it burning, a demanding job for the lighthouse keeper, and later for his assistant. The old lantern was the last light of its type used on the Pacific coast and was removed in 1947 after electricity was brought to the station. The Trinidad Head Lighthouse is still active, with a drum-type Fresnel lens in the tower and a backup modern beacon mounted outside the lantern room. A pair of fog signals are stacked next to the fog bell house, which is the only remaining bell house in California.

This photograph by photographer A. P. Flaglor shows Jeremiah Kiler, who was the lighthouse keeper for the Trinidad Head Lighthouse from 1871 to 1888. (Courtesy TMS, KB.)

This undated photograph shows the dwelling of the lighthouse keeper and his family at center, the lighthouse proper at left, and the bell house at lower right. (Courtesy HSU.)

This undated photograph was taken by R. J. Baker, a photographer who lived in the area between 1904 and 1908. It shows the fog alarm station perched at the edge of the Pacific Ocean off of Trinidad Head. The second lighthouse keeper, Fred L. Harrington, oversaw the installation in 1898 of the fog bell on the rocky outcrop roughly 50 feet below the level of the light. In 1947, the fog bell was replaced by compressed air horns. (Courtesy HCHS.)

This undated photograph shows the frame bell house that housed the clockwork mechanism for the alarm bell. Next to it is the tower for the weights, which descended down the face of the cliff and served to power the strike hammer. The 4,000-pound bell was struck at prescribed intervals by the heavy hammer. (Courtesy TMS, KB.)

This photograph shows lighthouse keeper Edward Wilborg (left) and assistant lighthouse keeper Malcolm Cady by the lighthouse automobile. Wilborg took over as head lighthouse keeper from Fred L. Harrington in 1916. (Courtesy TMS, KB.)

Assistant lighthouse keeper Malcolm Cady, who later became head lighthouse keeper, is shown with his fish catch by the lighthouse residences on Trinidad Head. (Courtesy TMS, KB.)

Boys pose on the water cistern of the residence at Trinidad Lighthouse. The white building shown belongs to the U.S. Coast Guard. The original dwelling was expanded to the size shown after the addition of the fog alarm bell in 1898. The keeper was required to wind the clock machinery every two hours. (Courtesy TMS, KB.)

This postcard photograph shows the Trinidad Lighthouse from below. The postmark date stamps show that it was sent as a New Year's greeting on January 4, 1908. (Courtesy HSU.)

This postcard shows the Great White Fleet passing Trinidad in 1908. In 1907, Pres. Teddy Roosevelt sent out a sizeable contingent of the U. S. fleet to circumnavigate the globe. Between May and July of 1908, the fleet undertook the second leg of the voyage, which was from San Francisco to Puget Sound and back. This prepared them for the third and final leg of the journey: from San Francisco to Hawaii, New Zealand, Australia, Japan, China, and ending in the Philippine Islands at Manila. (Courtesy HSU.)

This 1912 photograph shows the view out to sea from the cliff of Trinidad Head above the lighthouse residences. (Courtesy HSU.)

This photograph was taken by A. W. Ericson and shows the lighthouse from above. The lighthouse keeper is standing on the lighthouse deck and people are gathered on the promontory below. (Courtesy HCHS.)

In 1948, Earl Hallmark of the Hallmark Fisheries deeded land on the bluff overlooking Trinidad Bay to the Trinidad Civic Club for the Trinidad Memorial Lighthouse. In 1949, the lamp, with its clock mechanism and pedestal, and the original lens and fog bell were moved to the new site, which was opened on June 26, 1949. Attending the dedication ceremony were many notables including Gary Hunter, whose great-grandfather, Colonel Harrington, and father, Gary Hunter Sr., had been lighthouse keepers. Note that the dates written on the photograph are incorrect. (Courtesy HCHS.)

This 1949 photograph shows the Trinidad Memorial Lighthouse with Trinidad Head rising in the background. The memorial was designed by Trinidad's Edgar Allen Poe, no relation to his almost namesake. (Courtesy TMS.)

The anchor memorial was installed around 1972 and displays the dedication "To Those Who Have Lost Their Lives At Sea." The anchor is of the Danforth type used by World War II landing craft. It was reconditioned and painted by Ralph Hunter. (Courtesy HCHS.)

# *Four*

# TRINIDAD WHALING
# STATION

The *Humboldt Times* noted on September 23, 1854: "It's surprising with all the whales seen off-shore that no one has from this coast formed an association to catch whales." The suggestion of the writer was first realized in Humboldt County in 1855 when Capt. H. H. Buhne began to engage in whaling on his steamer, the *Mary Anne*, with many successful catches throughout the summer. The crew processed caught whales at Humboldt Point, later to be known as Buhne Point, near Fields Landing. Later that year, the Crescent Whaling Company started a whaling station on Whaler's Island in Crescent City. Abundant shark hunting briefly eclipsed the nascent local whaling industry, but two years later sharks were depleted and the primacy of whaling resumed.

The whalers' cry, "Tha'r she blows!" was frequently heard on whaling vessels operating out of Trinidad Bay starting in the early 1860s, when a station affiliated with the Crescent City station started in Trinidad. This station did not last long because of increasingly depleted stocks of the great sea mammals. Already depleted on the east coast, the west coast whaling industry, with San Francisco as its principal hub, saw a decline in whale populations by the 1880s. In the early 1900s, however, whaling revived with advances in harpoon technology and the multiplicity of commercial uses found for whale-based products. Capt. Frederick Dedrick started whaling operations at his California Sea Products Company at Moss Landing Harbor in 1919, and then expanded his operations by building the Trinidad Whaling Station in 1920. The Trinidad Whaling Station operated from 1920 to 1927. When whale populations again declined, California Sea Products Company closed its Moss Landing Harbor station in 1926 and its station at Trinidad Harbor in 1927. The era of Trinidad whaling had come to an end.

This photograph was taken on June 30, 1920, and shows the main whaling station under construction. Equipment to build the station was sent by train to the Trinidad Rail Depot nearby. However, transporting heavy equipment by truck from the depot to the station was very difficult. In one instance, a 32-ton dryer used in meat processing became stuck on a large redwood stump. Moving the dryer off the stump took most of a day to accomplish. (Courtesy TMS.)

This 1920 photograph shows the whaling ramp under construction by the Mercer Fraser Company. Old growth redwood timber was the main building material. Notice the horse team (back right) that was used to move large boards. The ramp was located in the same place as the Trinidad Dock between Trinidad Head and Little Head. (Courtesy TMS.)

This photograph shows the view from Golindo Street of the California Sea Products Company fertilizer during a fire. After processing, all remaining whale parts were ground and dried and put into sacks to be sold as fertilizer. (Courtesy TMS, BL.)

This photograph shows the Trinidad Whaling Station at the height of whaling operations. Many specialized structures for the rendering of whale products are shown. (Courtesy TMS, KB.)

This 1903 H. S. Hutchinson and Co. photograph shows Japanese workers cutting up sperm whale blubber aboard the bark *California* off the coast of Japan. Whaling was big business not just in Humboldt County, but around the world. (Courtesy Library of Congress.)

This undated photograph shows a couple of steamers in various stages of loading and unloading. Most whale products from the Trinidad Whaling Station were transported by train from the Trinidad Rail Depot operated by Northwestern Pacific. (Courtesy HCHS.)

Susie Baker Fountain took this photograph on April 27, 1924, which shows the ocean liner *Ruth Alexander* in Trinidad Bay. It was reported that while at anchor in Trinidad Bay, a floating object punctured the hull at the lower beam end. (Courtesy HSU.)

This photograph shows Mrs. Morton and her children (shown between the ladder beams, center right) on a platform near the whaling ramp in Trinidad. The family and others came to see the *Ruth Alexander* in distress with 233 passengers and a crew of 115 men, all of whom remained on board. (Courtesy HSU.)

This photograph shows the rare catch of a blue whale on the whaling ramp. In 1924, only a single blue whale catch was recorded. Blue whales were abundant until the beginning of the 20th century, when they were hunted nearly to extinction. Up to 100 feet long and weighing up to 150 tons, the blue whale is the largest animal that has ever lived on earth. The average blue whale is 70 feet long and weighs 100 tons. (Courtesy TMS, BL.)

This photograph shows the tail flukes of a whale as it travels beneath the whaler SS *Hawk*. Whaling was considered a dangerous operation, mostly attributable to sea conditions rather than the actions of whale prey. However, Herman Melville's famous tale of the great white whale *Moby Dick* was based on stories of a real whale, an albino sperm whale, that reputedly attacked whaling vessels and killed whalers. (Courtesy TMS, BL.)

This photograph shows crewmen's shadows along the back of a captured finback whale. Second in size only to the blue whale, the finback reaches about 70 feet in length and weighs up to 70 tons. It shares with the blue whale the distinction of having the deepest voice on earth. (Courtesy TMS, BL.)

This photograph shows Capt. Frederick Dedrick, a Norwegian whaler who in 1914 opened the California Sea Products Company in Moss Landing Harbor, where the Monterey Bay Aquarium Research Institute now stands, as well as in Trinidad Harbor. (Courtesy TMS, KB.)

This photograph shows the whaler SS *Hawk* in Trinidad Bay. On the bow is the harpoon gun. On the mast is the crow's nest, in which a man can stand as lookout for whales. The large smokestack indicates that this is a coal-burning vessel. (Courtesy TMS, BL.)

This photograph shows an SS *Hawk* crew member on the bow with the vessel's harpoon gun. Svend Foyn, a Norwegian sea captain, revolutionized the whaling industry by his invention of the modern harpoon gun, which consisted of a cannon that fired a barbed explosive-head harpoon. (Courtesy TMS, BL.)

This unusual photograph shows the gunner in firing position facing forward on the bow of the SS *Hawk*. After a whale was sighted, the ship would move in as close as possible to fire the harpoon gun. (Courtesy TMS, BL.)

This photograph shows the gunner for the SS *Hawk* posed in front of a large whale flipper. An entry in the log for June 1922 reports, "*Hawk* moored in Trinidad. In with two humps [humpbacks]; whales plentiful." (Courtesy TMS, BL.)

This photograph shows the crew of the SS *Hawk* standing on the deck. The captain, Julius Blatt, is shown at center. The man at his left is holding the ship's cat, Maggie. (Courtesy TMS, BL.)

This photograph shows two whalers standing on a whale alongside their vessel. After a harpooned whale was brought alongside the ship, it was pumped full of air, and then a buoy marker flag attached to it. The whale would be left floating until they retrieved it on the return trip to Trinidad Harbor. (Courtesy TMS, BL.)

Not all harpooned and flagged whales made it back to the harbor. The photograph above shows one that did: a finback whale starting its ascent up the whaling station ramp. One that did not make it is described in the whaling log of the other Trinidad whaler, the SS *Port Saunders*: "Lost two whales and four harpoons, Oct. 2, *Port Saunders* shot first whale 30 miles northwest of Trinidad, at 3:00 p.m. flagged same; at 6:00 p.m. shot second whale, started for flagged whale, when southeast gale came up, heavy sea, could not locate first whale, heavy sea and rain, sea so rough had to tow second whale astern with heavy towlines, towline gave way in heavy sea, unable to pick up whale again, lost same." The 1922 photograph below shows the full length of the ramp. The whalers SS *Hawk* and SS *Port Saunders* are shown returning to the harbor. (Courtesy TMS, BL and KB.)

This photograph shows a crowd gathered at the top of the whaling ramp. Note the flensing knife held by a worker standing at left and the excitement of the child exclaiming at right. The flensing knife or hook was used to strip the blubber from the whale. (Courtesy TMS, BL.)

This photograph shows a giant finback whale, open-mouthed, at the top of the whaling ramp at the Trinidad Whaling Station. Whales were hauled up the ramp with the assistance of a steam donkey engine, similar to that used for hauling logs. In 1926, the station recorded catches of 70 finback whales. (Courtesy TMS, BL.)

This undated photograph shows a whale being taken in to the harbor by the SS *Hawk*. Whales were typically anchored overnight in the harbor, and then hauled up the ramp at first light the following morning. (Courtesy TMS, BL.)

This photograph shows workers at the Trinidad Whaling Station standing amidst large squares of whale blubber after the whale has been flensed and the blubber cut into manageable pieces. At the end of the station's first season, on November 20, 1920, the only station fatality ever to occur happened. Hobert Haynes, 22 years old, was working with the cutting machine when one of the rapidly revolving blades flew off and decapitated him. (Courtesy TMS.)

This 1922 photograph by A. W. Ericson shows a humpback whale being hauled up the ramp into the whaling station. The photographer is shown walking up the ramp. Ericson would often set up his shots so that he could be in them. In 1926, the station recorded catches of 21 humpback whales. (Courtesy TMS, KB.)

This photograph shows four workers standing on a whale being hauled up the whaling ramp. At one time there were 60 employees at the station and the pay was considered better than average. Workers received room and board and lived at the large boarding house near the station. Wages averaged $30 a month with a $1.50 bonus for each whale brought in. (Courtesy TMS, BL.)

This 1922 photograph shows two men sitting on the underside of the mouth, head, and flippers of a humpback whale while another man looks on. One of the biggest problems experienced by station neighbors both locally and downwind was the foul odor. During the years that the station operated, a popular slogan was, "You can smell Trinidad before you can see it!" Workers reportedly became used to the odor. (Courtesy TMS, KB.)

This 1966 photograph shows concrete blocks constructed in 1921 for skidding whale carcasses up to the rendering plant. These are located near the Trinidad Dock. The last California Sea Products Company building to be dismantled was the former office building, razed in July 1961. (Courtesy HSU.)

This 1920s photograph shows the fishing fleet along with the two larger whaling boats. During this period, the Trinidad Harbor and the Trinidad Rail Depot were busy. In the first two years of Trinidad Whaling Station operation, the railroad shipped more than 200 carloads of oil and fertilizer. It also brought in more than 150 carloads of supplies, machinery, and fuel. (Courtesy HCHS, LS.)

This photograph shows head flenser Jack Money standing in front of a humpback whale. Flensing a whale required cutting it lengthwise into long strips. The meat was then cut into pieces and placed into a series of digesters and rendered. The end result was whale oil, which had many uses, including soaps and precision machinery. (Courtesy TMS, KB.)

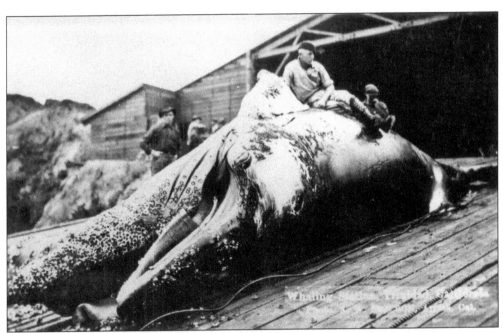

This photograph by A. W. Ericson shows a man sitting atop a humpback whale. Most of the whale oil produced at the Trinidad Whaling Station was purchased by Procter and Gamble for its Ivorydale factory. William Procter, a candlemaker, and James Gamble, a soapmaker, formed the company known as Procter and Gamble in 1837. Over time, the company began to focus most of its attention on soap, producing more than 30 different types by the 1890s. (Courtesy TMS, KB.)

This photograph shows a fog-enshrouded whaling ship near the whaling ramp at the Trinidad Whaling Station. Men hurry down to the whale carcass to attach the cables that will help them haul it up to the station. Notice the large redwood vat at left. (Courtesy TMS, BL.)

The Trinidad Whaling Station saw many whales—finback, humpback, gray, sei, sperm, and even a single blue—cross its redwood decks to be rendered into oil and dried into fertilizer. Workers came from all over, responding to help wanted signs in cities like San Francisco, seeking wages and adventure. When whale populations began to plummet and the price of whale oil decreased, it became too expensive to operate the station, which closed in 1927. Workers who wished to stay in the area had only fishing and logging to turn to for jobs. The whales traveling in the waters off Trinidad were given a reprieve from hunting at last. That is, until 1938, when Maritime Industries set up a whaling station at Fields Landing, and the hunt resumed. In 1951, the last whaling station in Humboldt County closed—this time for good. In the words of poet Gary Snyder: *The whales turn and glisten, plunge / and sound and rise again, / Hanging over subtly darkening deeps / Flowing like breathing planets / in the sparkling whorls of / living light.* (Courtesy TMS, BL.)

# Five

# TRINIDAD LOGGING AND CRANNELL

The coast redwood, *Sequoia sempervirens*, once covered much of the planet. Fossil remains have been found in Alaska and Greenland as well as in most of the continental United States and Europe. However, by the time Spanish and English explorers were making landings on California's coast in the 16th through the early-19th centuries, the coast redwood's range was restricted to the northern California coast and just over the border into Oregon. In the 1850s, Baron von Loeffelholz operated a mill at what is today known as Luffenholtz Creek south of Trinidad. Deming and March built a mill on Mill Creek on the north side of Trinidad. In 1869, Smith and Doughety built a mill. The Hooper brothers, who eventually owned both the Deming and March mill and the Smith and Doughety mill, became the town's major employer with both of their mills fully staffed as the newly formed Trinidad Mill Company. In 1883, the Trinidad Mill Company was sold to the California Redwood Company syndicate, whose holdings included most of the timber from the Humboldt Bay up to Redwood Creek. Mule and oxen skid roads became railbeds as railroads were built to follow the timber. Loggers and mill workers followed the jobs, first in the forests directly adjacent to Trinidad, and then further out. Crannell was the company logging town of the Little River Redwood Company and it employed many workers from Trinidad. During its heyday (1923–1931), Crannell was an end-to-end logging operation, logging the woods that it owned, milling the timber on site, and then shipping out finished lumber to market. In 1931, after merging with the Hammond Lumber Company, the Crannell mill was shut down and all logs were shipped to the Hammond Mill at Samoa. In spite of this, Crannell continued to thrive and at its height had 450 residents and over 100 homes. After the 1945 fire and the shift to logging the Big Lagoon Tract, Georgia Pacific Company acquired Hammond Lumber Company in 1956. In 1969, Georgia Pacific decided to remove the last traces of Crannell, which marked the end of northern Humboldt's last quintessential company logging town.

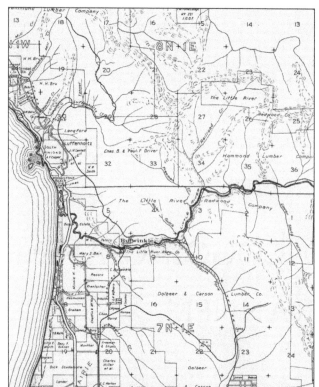

When this map was published in 1921, Crannell was known as Bulwinkle. Most of the land at this time was still covered with virgin redwood forest that had once been public land but was by then privately held by various lumber companies. Little River Redwood Company was incorporated in 1892 and later merged with the Lagoon Lumber Company in 1923. The history of Lagoon Lumber went back to the California Redwood Company in which Scottish investors illegally purchased tens of thousands of acres in Little River, Trinidad, Maple Creek, and Big Lagoon. (Courtesy HCHS.)

This 1886 photograph by A. W. Gilfillan shows a team of 10 horses and mules hauling logs out of the logged-over woods north of Trinidad. (Courtesy TMS, KB.)

This *c.* 1928 photograph shows a portion of the 30,000 acres of the Big Lagoon Tract. It was taken from the air at an elevation of 3,000 feet. In 1947, Hammond shifted its logging efforts from areas near Crannell to the Big Lagoon Tract north of Trinidad. (Courtesy CL.)

This 1880 photograph by A. W. Ericson shows an oxen team pulling logs on a skid trail. Although skid trail logging by oxen were eventually replaced by railroad logging, oxen teams continued to be used until 1915. Skid roads took a lot of work to build. After placing the logs, the area between the logs was filled to provide an even footing for the oxen. Costs per mile were as high as $5,000. (Courtesy TMS, KB.)

This 1885 photograph, taken in the Trinidad area, shows men posed on a large log that is cabled up, ready to be pulled along the skid row. To ease the way for oxen teams or horse-powered hauling, wooden bridges were often built to make the land level. This also made it easier for the woodsmen. (Courtesy TMS, KB.)

This photograph shows the unloading of logs up a ramp with a screw jack and donkey engine, the latter barely visible at far right. Every logging company had its own design of screw jacks. (Courtesy TMS, KB.)

This 1885 photograph shows lunchtime at a logging site east of Trinidad. The steam donkey engine shown was the preferred overland method for moving the giant logs to rivers or railroads that were often many miles away. (Courtesy TMS, KB.)

This 1906 A. W. Ericson photograph shows Bulwinkle at the site of the former John Bullwinkel homestead at the beginning of mill construction. A later Ericson photograph shows Bulwinkle as a onestack mill with cookhouses, office, pedestrian bridge, and a railroad bridge, all of which replaced the initial ranch. (Courtesy TMS, KB.)

Redwood Logs - Little River Redwood Co. Bulwinkle Calif. Bliler Fortuna

This postcard, with a faded Bulwinkle postmark, shows a locomotive in Bulwinkle pulling sections of giant redwoods, one per railcar. In September 1922, the town of Bulwinkle was renamed Crannell in honor of the Little River Redwood Company president, Levi Crannell of Canada. (Courtesy HHS, LS.)

This 1916 postcard shows a logging train on a trestle above Bulwinkle. Francis Wible's two-cylinder 1907 REO car is also shown. By the 1930s, when logs were milled at the Hammond Company mill at Samoa, logs taken from the company woods would travel the mostly flat grade from Crannell to Samoa, along the sand dunes of Clam Beach, and over the Mad River railroad bridge. (Courtesy TMS, KB.)

This c. 1920s photograph shows the Camp 13 trestle located near the 25 Junction of the Hammond and Little River Railroad Company railroad. Once the flatcars were loaded in the woods, they would be pulled to Crannell for processing. After the Crannell mill closed in 1931, the flatcars would be taken two or three at a time to the mill at Samoa. (Courtesy TMS, KB.)

This A. W. Ericson photograph shows Engine No. 11 with 20 carloads of redwood timber, heading south on the Luffenholtz trestle. The photograph was taken from present day Skyhorse Ranch Lane. The locomotive is a 2-8-0 steam locomotive that was said to start and move "impressive loads at unimpressive speeds." (Courtesy TMS, KB.)

This early-1900s photograph shows a partially completed logging camp and the train transport of several half-cabins. Logging camps would be set up, lived in, and moved after logging to the next patch of intact forest to repeat the process. (Courtesy TMS, LS.)

This 1910 photograph shows cooks Annie Kirkpatrick (left) and Marie Reeves (Peters), both wearing hats and standing outside the California Barrel Company logging camp at Essex/Dows Prairie. Peters was the niece of John Bullwinkel. (Courtesy TMS, KB.)

This 1920 photograph looks west from Hammond Camp 21, approximately 3 miles east of Trinidad, and not far from the earlier Camp 7. (Courtesy TMS, KB.)

This 1910 photograph shows a survey crew of five men at Camp 18, near Little River. (Courtesy TMS, KB.)

This *c.* 1920 Freeman Art photograph shows four rows of men in front of a giant redwood undercut at Hammond Camp 20. Camp 20 was 5.2 miles northeast of Crannell. (Courtesy TMS, KB.)

This 1910 photograph shows a yarding crew at Hammond Camp 10 posed by a steam yarder. From the rails in the woods, they sent the logs to Samoa. Camp 10 was in the upper Little River watershed northeast of Crannell and not far from Maple Creek. (Courtesy TMS, KB.)

This 1930 aerial photograph shows the three-stack mill in operation. Two major fires, in 1908 and 1945, frame the beginning and the end of Crannell. Following extensive logging by the Hammond Lumber Company, the 1908 fire at Luffenholtz devastated the area from Little River to Trinidad, although it spared the newly built Little River Redwood Company mill at Bulwinkle. Through a series of mergers and acquisitions, the newly reincorporated Little River Redwood Company logged the Little River Tract along its many rail lines. (Courtesy TMS, TS.)

This 1928 photograph shows the view from the upper end of the Little River Redwood Company log pond as well as the saw mill and machine shop. When a second catastrophic fire in 1945 destroyed the system of railroad trestles, this marked the transition to hauling logs by truck and also started the final decline of Crannell. (Courtesy CL.)

Loggers used specialized tools for handling the giant redwoods. A pair of choppers might use a double-bitted axe and a 12-foot saw, called a misery whip, to cut a tree. During the 1920s, when this photograph was taken, the first step after felling a redwood was ringing the tree in preparation for peeling off the thick bark. Shown is a tree partly peeled with peeler bars. (Courtesy TMS, KB.)

This postcard photograph by A. W. Ericson shows loggers bucking a large redwood for shingle bolts in the Vance Woods in the 1880s. Shingle bolts are shown piled in the photograph's foreground. (Courtesy HCHS, LS.)

This 1928 photograph, from a Little River Redwood Company promotional booklet, shows a log 10 feet in diameter and 20 feet long at the foot of the log slip. According to the brochure, "The man with the long pike pole is Tommy James, head pond man, a full-blooded Klamath Indian. He has been with the company for over 16 years." (Courtesy CL.)

This 1928 photograph shows a log that is nine feet in diameter on the log slip on its way to the mill. E. A. Harvey, the machine shop foreman, is shown standing on the runway. (Courtesy CL.)

This 1928 photograph shows an unidentified mill worker standing in front of a log that is nine feet in diameter. The log is in position on the carriage of the No. 1 band mill. It scaled 10,562 board feet measure. (Courtesy CL.)

This photograph shows the log deck with band mill No. 1 at right and No. 2 at left. The log on carriage No. 1 is headed toward edgers and trimmers. (Courtesy CL.)

This 1928 photograph shows the huge sorting table sheds at Little River Redwood Company in Crannell. A monorail and transfer crane system for loading lumber is located at the back of the mill. (Courtesy CL.)

This 1928 photograph shows nearly finished lumber stacked in the planing mill at Little River Redwood Company in Crannell. (Courtesy CL.)

This photograph shows Ken Cole (right) and an unidentified friend on the speeder, a type of homemade car to be used in an area with no roads. Cole came to Bulwinkle as a child with his parents and family. While he was growing up, his father worked for the Little River Redwood Company. As an adult, Cole went to work as an engineer for the rival company, Hammond, across Little River to the north. The two companies merged in 1931. (Courtesy TMS, KB.)

This 1924 photograph shows a high straddler carrier for lumber made by Williamette Iron and Steel Works. The carrier is in front of the dry shed at Little River Redwood Company in Crannell. (Courtesy TMS, KB.)

This photograph was taken in the 1920s by J. B. Andrews and shows the Hammond Lumber Company shop crew. Thomas A. Fulkerson is shown at right. He was reported to be the first in the county to use an acetylene settling torch. (Courtesy TMS, KB.)

This undated photograph shows a couple posing on a railroad bridge near Crannell. (Courtesy TMS, TS.)

This 1928 photograph shows houses on the hillside in Crannell. The east side of Crannell was called Hillside Terrace and the lower, west side was called Eucalyptus Heights. (Courtesy CL.)

This 1928 photograph shows the houses of company workers situated on a quiet, tree-lined street in Crannell. The town had family housing, bunkhouses, and a lodge for unmarried workers, a company store, grammar school, church, and even a fireman's dance hall. (Courtesy CL.)

This 1930 photograph shows students of Mrs. Clough (far left) on the wooden playground at Crannell. When the school closed in 1950, teacher Katie Boyle moved from Crannell to Trinidad. (Courtesy TMS, KB.)

This photograph, taken on May 10, 1913, shows a commemoration celebration in Bulwinkle. Lillian Estelle Sharp is shown at left with a dark coat. On the other side of the table sits Craigie S. Sharp at right with his daughter Frances Jane Sharp next to him. (Courtesy TMS, TS.)

This photograph shows the Little River Redwood Company store, a large two-story building that contained a department store, groceries, a meat counter, and the town's post office. At the end of the store building were the offices for the woods managers, safety, and payroll. (Courtesy TMS, TS.)

This September 1931 photograph shows Ken Cole's band Californians at Clam Beach. Shown left to right are Versal Cole, Ken Cole, Clearman Cole, and Jack Trego. Mrs. Trego, who played piano, is shown standing. (Courtesy TMS, KB.)

Hammond Lumber Company had its own scrip money, from a copper dollar to a penny in value. Each coin had an "H" stamped through it. If a worker needed to, he could borrow company scrip from the payroll office. (Courtesy TMS, TS.)

Wes Walch remembers that next to the store there was a barber shop, the bachelor men's cabins, a one-room library, and the large busy cookhouse. Walch grew up in Crannell and later became managing director of another company town owned by Weyerhauser. (Courtesy TMS, TS.)

This is the front of Crannell's former dining hall as it looked in 1966 when this photograph was taken. Like all buildings in Crannell, the dining hall was made entirely out of redwood lumber. Sidewalks, picket fences, water tanks, and bridges were all made from redwood boards or timbers. (Courtesy TMS, KB.)

This 1966 photograph shows the home of Crannell's head cook, Tony Gabriel, across from the former dining hall. Workers had large pancake breakfasts, box lunches for the woods crew, and big, prepared meals—all for about $30 a month. (Courtesy TMS, KB.)

*Six*

# TRINIDAD TODAY

Trinidad has become a popular tourist destination, with its beautiful view of the Pacific Ocean and many restaurants, shops, and bed-and-breakfast inns. The collection of photographs from the contemporary period shows Trinidad as a vibrant and friendly community. The Trinidad Museum is housed in a restored 1899–1900 Victorian Italianate bungalow, referred to as the Sangster-Watkins-Underwood house, which houses many rare artifacts from Trinidad's history. Annual events pictured, such as the Clam Beach Run, the Fish Festival, the Cockeyed Florence Parade, and the Blessing of the Fleet, make today's Trinidad a fun place for residents and visitors alike.

This 2007 photograph shows councilman Mike Morgan with Glenn and Janis Saunders on the day of the Fish Festival. The Saunders family has been central to Trinidad's character and development for decades. Their many contributions include their work as owners of Saunders Market, saving the Holy Trinity Catholic Church from demolition, serving on Trinidad City Council (Glenn was mayor), and donating the land near their home for the Trinidad Museum, Trinidad Library, and Saunders Park site. (Courtesy Mike Morgan.)

This aerial photograph from 1959 shows the many boats in the Trinidad Bay and the long Trinidad Dock jutting out between Trinidad Head and Little Head. (Courtesy TMS.)

This photograph was taken in June 1960, when the grading of the new freeway between Moonstone Beach and Trinidad was being completed. After the new Highway 101 was completed, the Old Redwood Highway was renamed Trinidad Scenic Drive. (Courtesy HSU.)

This photograph shows the dedication of the Saunders' property to the Humboldt North Coast Land Trust in July 2004. Shown left to right are Janis and Glenn Saunders and Mickey Fleschner. (Courtesy TMS.)

This 1973 photograph shows the Holy Trinity Church in its centennial year. The church building, constructed of high-grade redwood lumber, was meticulously restored and services are still held there today. (Courtesy TMS, KB.)

The Trinidad to Clam Beach Run began as a winter training race for Humboldt State University runners. It has evolved into a nationally known run. One unique feature of the run is crossing the mouth of the Little River at Moonstone Beach. The date and start time of the race are determined by the height of the tide on either the last Saturday of January or the first Saturday of February. (Courtesy TMS, KB.)

Longtime Trinidad resident Bill Devall is shown here in Big Flat in the King Range. Devall was professor emeritus of sociology at Humboldt State University, having taught courses in sociology and wide-ranging topics in environmental studies, including wilderness and forest protection and the effects of radioactive wastes. His first book, *Deep Ecology*, co-authored by George Sessions and published in 1985, introduced the philosophy and practice of deep ecology to a North American audience. This philosophy was described by Devall as "Earth wisdom—the dance of unity of plants, animals, humans, and the earth." Subsequent books discuss how to put his ideas into practice. Devall also edited *Clear Cut: The Tragedy of Industrial Forestry* (1995), and served on the advisory board for the 11-volume *Selected Works of Arne Naess*. In 2008, he published his final book, *The Ecology of Wisdom*. Devall was a founding member of the North Coast Environmental Center in Arcata, a leader of the Foundation of Deep Ecology, and an active participant in many other environmental groups, including the Ecostery Foundation in Victoria, British Columbia, and the Environmental Protection and Information Center in Garberville. (Courtesy Arcata Zen Center.)

This 1945 photograph shows Grace and Burr McConnaha. In 1903, Burr McConnaha owned and operated a stage line from Trinidad to Requa. (Courtesy TMS, KB.)

This photograph shows Trinity Street looking northwest. The home on the left is Dave Zebo's remodeled Sangster house. The Flying Bridge Café is shown at center. Flying Bridge Café is now the Trinidad Eatery. The power poles were removed in 1990. (TMS, KB.)

This photograph shows environmental activists Tim McKay and Lucille Vinyard at the Northcoast Environmental Center in 1981. A longtime Trinidad resident, Vinyard spoke in 1965 before the Senate Natural Resources Committee in Sacramento in support of establishing Redwood National Park to preserve the last of the ancient redwoods. Her impassioned 12-minute presentation received thunderous applause. From then on, Vinyard has voiced her support of wilderness before many government agencies and groups. She continues her conservation work with the Sierra Club North Group. A longtime resident of Westhaven, Tim McKay was the founder of the Northcoast Environmental Center in Arcata and fought to conserve forests, rivers, and fish. Major issues that McKay worked on include the Gasquet-Orleans Road (GO Road), northern spotted owl conservation, the establishment of the Siskiyou Wilderness, the Headwaters Forest Preserve, and the Klamath River restoration—particularly the ongoing fight to remove the Klamath dams. (Courtesy HSU, McKay Collection.)

This 1969 photograph shows the Trinidad Bay Smoke House on Golindo Street (now Galindo Street). (Courtesy TMS, KB.)

This 1960 photograph shows Katy's Sea Foods, precursor to Katy's Smokehouse, which still provides fresh salmon and sea foods to customers in Trinidad and beyond. (Courtesy TMS, KB.)

Martha Underwood is shown in her lush garden in 1950. Martha Underwood was a Watkins and was the daughter of Rose Ann McDonald Watkins Sangster, one of three early pioneer women of Trinidad. Her home has now been meticulously restored and is the new home of the Trinidad Museum. (Courtesy TMS.)

Located off Main Street and Patrick's Point Drive, the home of the Trinidad Museum is a restored 1899–1900 Victorian Italianate bungalow, referred to as the Sangster-Watkins-Underwood house. The house was donated by the family of Ernie and Gwyneth Susan, descendants of the original owners, and was moved from its original site near Trinidad State Beach to land donated by Glenn and Janis Saunders in September 2006. (Courtesy Ron Johnson.)

This 1961 photograph shows the banner installation for the annual Trinidad Crab Feed, sponsored by the Greater Trinidad Chamber of Commerce. Putting up the banner (left to right) are Fred Matthias, Jim Dickinson, Tom Odom, and Glenn Saunders. (Courtesy TMS.)

This 1950s photograph by Art Ray shows men dumping crabs in a live box at the Trinidad wharf. (Courtesy TMS, KB.)

This 1967 photograph shows to two unidentified men enjoying their crab feast at the annual Trinidad Crab Feed. (Courtesy TMS, KB.)

This 1967 aerial photograph shows the annual Trinidad Crab Feed being held at the Trinidad fire station. (Courtesy TMS, KB.)

This 1979 photograph shows the homes in southwest Trinidad. Edwards and Van Wycke Streets are shown running east-west along the bluffs. (Courtesy TMS, KB.)

Located on a bluff overlooking the Pacific Ocean in Trinidad, the Humboldt State University Marine Laboratory opened in 1965 and was established to provide a center for marine and environmental science teaching and research. The laboratory provides ready access to the local marine environments of rocky shorelines, sandy beach, and offshore kelp beds. (Courtesy Dione F. Armand.)

This 1964 photograph shows a fisherman netting his salmon catch. On Saturday, July 11, 1964, Robert Hallmark of Bob's Boat Basin at the Trinidad dock said that 474 salmon came in from the 100 sport boats that were out fishing; making it a record four fish to a boat. (Courtesy TMS.)

This undated postcard photograph taken by photographer Art Ray exhorts visitors to "romp in the sunshine and bathe in the surf at Scotty's Free Camp at Moonstone Beach on Redwood Highway." (Courtesy HCHS, LS.)

"Romp in the sunshine and bathe in the surf" at Scotty's Free Camp at Moonstone Beach on Redwood Highway.

This photograph was taken at the annual Trinidad Blessing of the Fleet held on Thanksgiving Day in 1996. Marge Zebo O'Brien is shown speaking to the assembled crowd on the Trinidad dock. (Courtesy TMS.)

This photograph shows Agate Beach in Patrick's Point State Park. The California State Parks Commission purchased Patrick's Point in 1929 after approval of the 1928 park bond. Additional land was acquired over several years, bringing the park's total to 640 acres. Patrick's Point State Park features a shoreline that ranges from the broad sandy stretch of Agate Beach to sheer cliffs that rise high above the sea. (Courtesy Dione F. Armand.)

This undated postcard photograph taken by photographer Art Ray shows many men out digging for clams at Clam Beach, south of Trinidad. (Courtesy HCHS, LS.)

This undated photograph shows boys taking a boat out into the surf at Moonstone Beach. (Courtesy HCHS, LS.)

This photograph was taken by Paul Thistleton on June 11, 1995, and shows Axel Lindgren Jr. (left) and Lindy Linberg at the Trinidad Fish Festival. (Courtesy TMS.)

This 1986 photograph shows Bonnie Lindgren at the original Trinidad Museum, demonstrating traditional Yurok basketry. (Courtesy TMS.)

This 2008 photograph shows Ned Simmons acting as master of ceremonies at the Cockeyed Florence Parade, which wends through Trinidad each year to celebrate at the Trinidad Cemetery. The event honors Florence, who because of her tarnished reputation was denied proper burial within the cemetery by judgmental townspeople. (Courtesy Rambling Jack's Laboratory.)

This photograph shows the North Coast Bag Pipe Band performing on Edwards Street during the 1996 Fish Festival. The restored town hall building is shown on the right. (Courtesy TMS.)

Visit us at
arcadiapublishing.com